Name ____

MW00977218

Cost	Product Costs				
	Direct Materials Cost	Direct Labor Cost	Factory Overhead Cost	Selling Expense	Administrative Expense
a.					
b.					
c.					
d.					
e.					
f.					
g.					
h.					
i.					
j.					
k.					
l.					
m.					
n.					
o.					
p.					
q.					
r.					
s.					
t.					
u.					
v.					
w.					
x.					
y.					
z.					

Page Not Used.

Name ____________________

PROBLEM 14 - 2 ___

JOURNAL

PAGE

	DATE		DESCRIPTION	POST. REF.	DEBIT	CREDIT	
1							1
2							2
3							3
4							4
5							5
6							6
7							7
8							8
9							9
10							10
11							11
12							12
13							13
14							14
15							15
16							16
17							17
18							18
19							19
20							20
21							21
22							22
23							23
24							24
25							25
26							26
27							27
28							28
29							29
30							30
31							31
32							32
33							33

PROBLEM 14 - 2 ___ , Concluded

JOURNAL

PAGE

DATE		DESCRIPTION	POST. REF.	DEBIT	CREDIT

Name ______________________________

PROBLEM 14 - 3 ___

1.

JOURNAL

PAGE

	DATE		DESCRIPTION	POST. REF.	DEBIT	CREDIT	
1							1
2							2
3							3
4							4
5							5
6							6
7							7
8							8
9							9
10							10
11							11
12							12
13							13
14							14
15							15
16							16
17							17
18							18
19							19
20							20
21							21
22							22
23							23
24							24
25							25
26							26
27							27
28							28
29							29
30							30
31							31
32							32
33							33

PROBLEM 14 - 3 ___ , Concluded

2.

Work in Process

Finished Goods

3.

Schedule of Unfinished Jobs

	DIRECT MATERIALS	DIRECT LABOR	FACTORY OVERHEAD	TOTAL

4.

Schedule of Completed Jobs

	DIRECT MATERIALS	DIRECT LABOR	FACTORY OVERHEAD	TOTAL

Name ____________________

PROBLEM 14 - 4 ___

JOB ORDER COST SHEET

Customer	____________________	Date	____________________
Address	____________________	Date wanted	____________________
	____________________	Date completed	____________________
Item	____________________	Job No.	____________________

ESTIMATE

Direct Materials		Direct Labor		Summary	
	Amount		Amount		Amount
___meters at $ ___	______	___hours at $ ___	______	Direct materials	______
___meters at ___	______	___hours at ___	______	Direct labor	______
___meters at ___	______	___hours at ___	______	Factory overhead	______
___meters at ___	______	___hours at ___	______	Total cost	______
Total	______	Total	______		

ACTUAL

Direct Materials			Direct Labor			Summary	
Mat. Req. No.	Description	Amount	Time Ticket No.	Description	Amount	Item	Amount
___	______	______	___	______	______	Direct materials	______
___	______	______	___	______	______	Direct labor	______
___	______	______	___	______	______	Factory overhead	______
___	______	______	___	______	______	Total cost	______
Total		______	Total		______		

Comments:

Page Not Used.

Name ______________________________

PROBLEM 14 - 5 ___

PROBLEM 14 - 5 ___ , Concluded

Name ____________________

PROBLEM 14 - 6 ___

1.

PROBLEM 14 - 6 ___ , Concluded

2.

Name ____________________

PROBLEM 15 - 1 ___

1.

JOURNAL

PAGE

	DATE		DESCRIPTION	POST. REF.	DEBIT	CREDIT	
1							1
2							2
3							3
4							4
5							5
6							6
7							7
8							8
9							9
10							10
11							11
12							12
13							13
14							14
15							15
16							16
17							17
18							18
19							19
20							20
21							21
22							22
23							23
24							24
25							25
26							26
27							27
28							28
29							29
30							30
31							31
32							32
33							33

PROBLEM 15 - 1 ___ , Concluded

JOURNAL

PAGE

	DATE		DESCRIPTION	POST. REF.	DEBIT	CREDIT	
1							1
2							2
3							3
4							4
5							5
6							6

2. and 3.

Name ____________________

PROBLEM 15 - 2 ___

JOURNAL

PAGE

	DATE	DESCRIPTION	POST. REF.	DEBIT	CREDIT	
1						1
2						2
3						3
4						4
5						5
6						6
7						7
8						8
9						9
10						10
11						11
12						12
13						13
14						14
15						15
16						16
17						17
18						18
19						19
20						20
21						21
22						22
23						23
24						24
25						25
26						26
27						27
28						28
29						29
30						30
31						31
32						32
33						33

PROBLEM 15 - 2 ___ , Concluded

JOURNAL

PAGE

	DATE		DESCRIPTION	POST. REF.	DEBIT	CREDIT	
1							1
2							2
3							3
4							4
5							5
6							6
7							7
8							8
9							9
10							10
11							11
12							12
13							13
14							14
15							15
16							16
17							17
18							18
19							19
20							20
21							21
22							22
23							23
24							24
25							25
26							26
27							27
28							28
29							29
30							30
31							31
32							32
33							33

Name ____________________

PROBLEM 15 - 3 ___

UNITS	WHOLE UNITS	EQUIVALENT UNITS	
		DIRECT MATERIALS	CONVERSION

PROBLEM 15 - 3 ___ , Concluded

COSTS	COSTS		
	DIRECT MATERIALS	CONVERSION	TOTAL COSTS

Name ______________________________

PROBLEM 15 - 4 ___

1.

UNITS	WHOLE UNITS	EQUIVALENT UNITS	
		DIRECT MATERIALS	CONVERSION

PROBLEM 15 - 4 ___ , Continued

COSTS	COSTS		
	DIRECT MATERIALS	CONVERSION	TOTAL COSTS

Name ______________________________

PROBLEM 15 - 4 ___ , Continued

2.

JOURNAL

PAGE ______

DATE		DESCRIPTION	POST. REF.	DEBIT	CREDIT

PROBLEM 15 - 4 ___ , Concluded

3.

Name ______________________________

PROBLEM 15 - 5 ___

1. and 2.

ACCOUNT *Work in Process—_______________ Department* ACCOUNT NO.

DATE		ITEM	POST. REF.	DEBIT	CREDIT	BALANCE	
						DEBIT	CREDIT

PROBLEM 15 - 5 ___ , Continued

1.

UNITS	WHOLE UNITS	EQUIVALENT UNITS	
		DIRECT MATERIALS	CONVERSION

Name ____________________

PROBLEM 15 - 5 ___ , Continued

COSTS	COSTS		
	DIRECT MATERIALS	CONVERSION	TOTAL COSTS

PROBLEM 15 - 5 ___ , Continued

2.

UNITS	WHOLE UNITS	EQUIVALENT UNITS	
		DIRECT MATERIALS	CONVERSION

Name ______________________________

PROBLEM 15 - 5 ___ , Concluded

COSTS	COSTS		
	DIRECT MATERIALS	CONVERSION	TOTAL COSTS

Page Not Used.

Name ____________________

PROBLEM 16 - 1 ___

Cost	Fixed Cost	Variable Cost	Mixed Cost
a.			
b.			
c.			
d.			
e.			
f.			
g.			
h.			
i.			
j.			
k.			
l.			
m.			
n.			
o.			
p.			
q.			
r.			
s.			
t.			

Page Not Used.

Name ______________________________

PROBLEM 16 - 2 ___

1. *Omit "00" in the cents columns.*

	FIXED COSTS	VARIABLE COSTS

2. through 8.

PROBLEM 16 - 2 ___ , Concluded

Name ______________________________

PROBLEM 16 - 3 ___

1. and 2.

PROBLEM 16 - 3 ___ , Concluded

3.

Sales and Costs

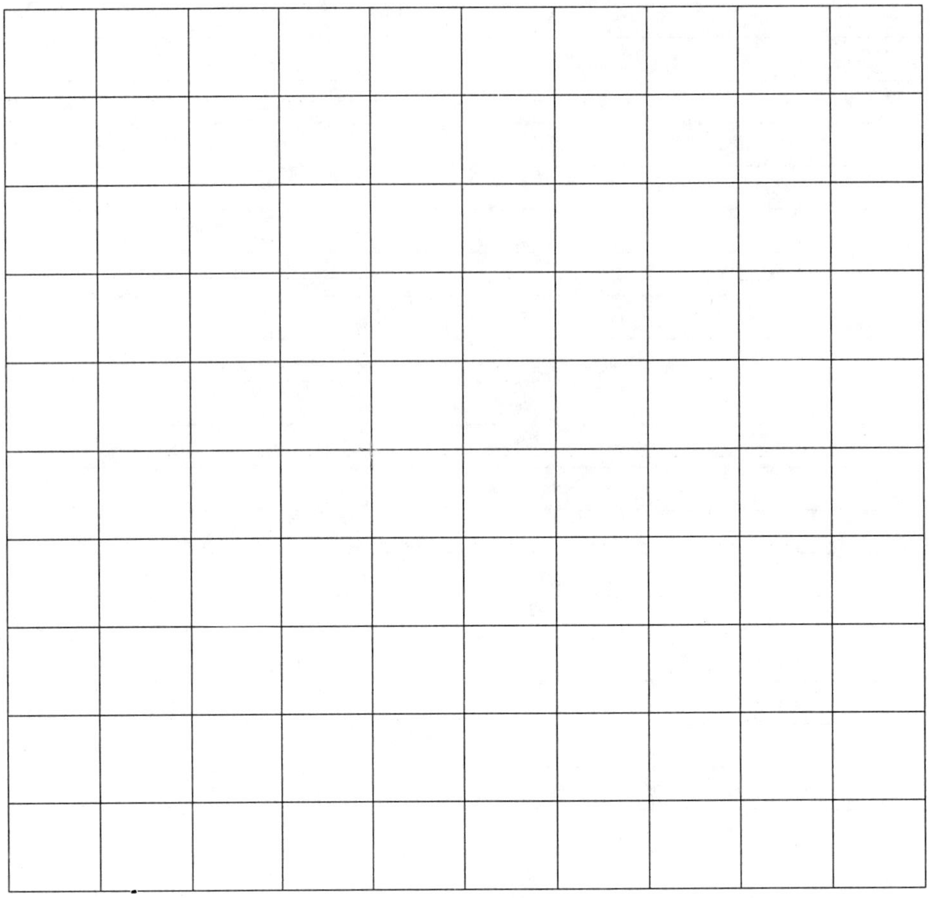

Units of Sales

4.

Name ______________________________

PROBLEM 16 - 4 ___

1.

Sales and Costs

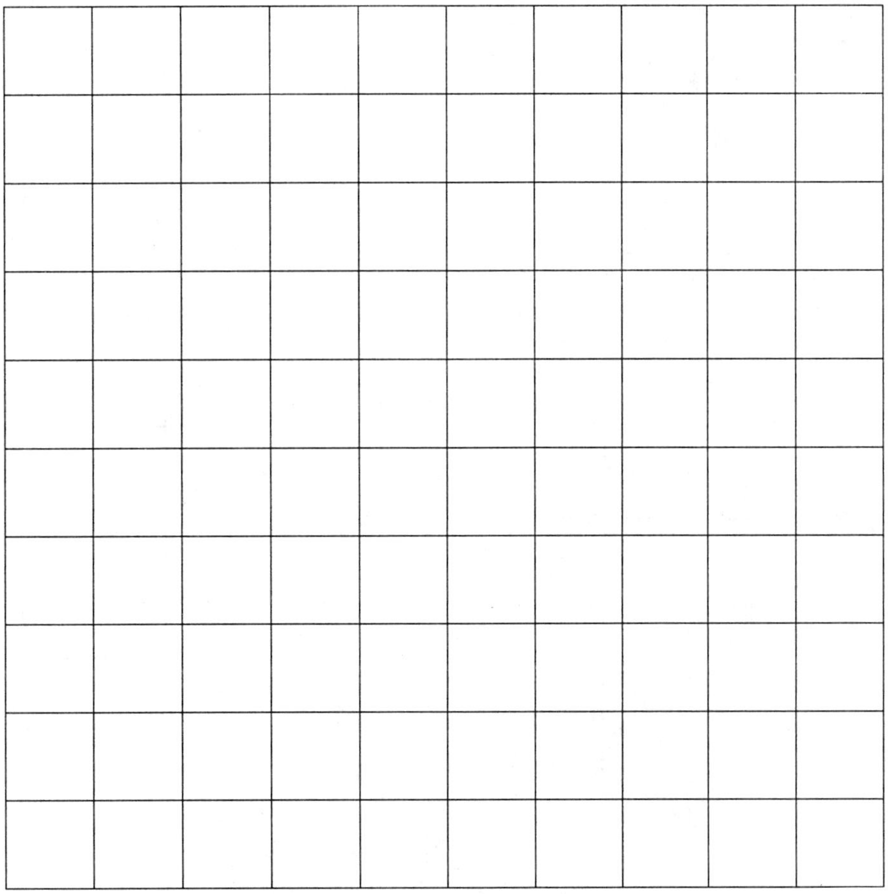

Units of Sales

2.a. ______________________________

b. ______________________________

3.

Sales and Costs

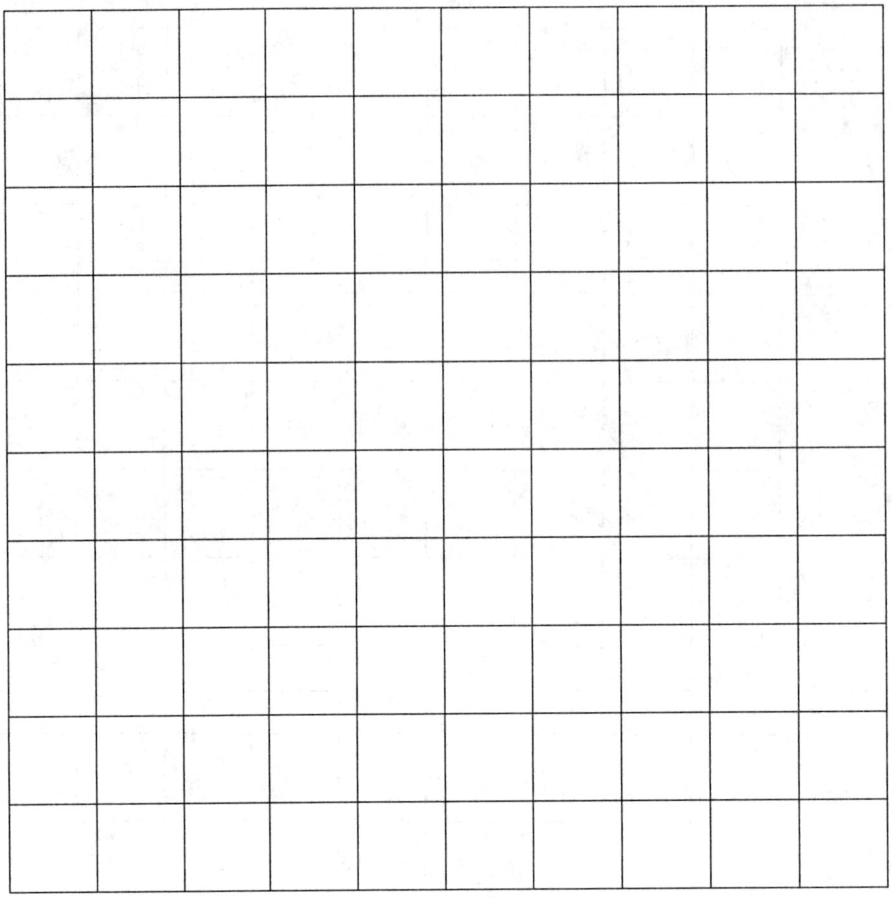

Units of Sales

4.a. ______________________________

b. ______________________________

Name ______________________________

PROBLEM 16 - 5 ___

PROBLEM 16 - 5 ___ , Concluded

Name ____________________

PROBLEM 16 - 6 ___

1. *Omit "00" in the cents columns.*

Estimated Income Statement

For Year Ending December 31, 2000

PROBLEM 16 - 6 ___ , Continued

2. and 3.

4.

Sales and Costs

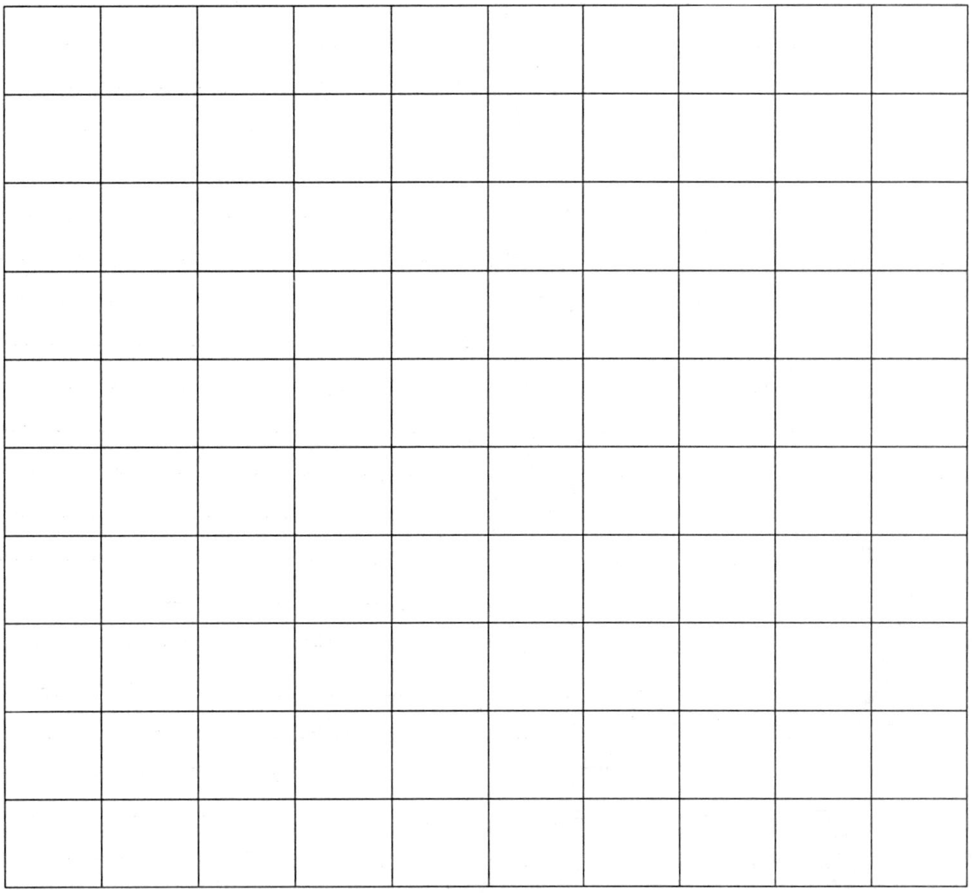

Units of Sales

PROBLEM 16 - 6 ___ , Concluded

5. and 6.

Name ____________________

PROBLEM 17 - 1 ___

1. *Omit "00" in the cents column.*

2.

PROBLEM 17 - 1 ___ , Concluded

3.

Name ______________________________

PROBLEM 17 - 2 ___

1. *Omit "00" in the cents column.*

2.

PROBLEM 17 - 2 ___ , Concluded

3.

4.

Name ______________________

PROBLEM 17 - 3 ___

1. a. *Omit "00" in the cents column.*

1. b.

PROBLEM 17 - 3 ___ , Continued

2. a.

2. b.

3.

PROBLEM 17 - 3 ___ , Concluded

4.

Name ____________________

PROBLEM 17 - 4 ___

1.

SALESPERSON	CONTRIBUTION MARGIN	VARIABLE COST OF GOODS SOLD AS A PERCENT OF SALES	VARIABLE SELLING EXPENSES AS A PERCENT OF SALES	CONTRIBUTION MARGIN RATIO

2.

PROBLEM 17 - 4 ___ , Concluded

3.

Name ______________________________

PROBLEM 17 - 5 ___

1. *Omit "00" in the cents column.*

	SIZE			TOTAL
	S	M	L	

2.

PROBLEM 17 - 5 ___ , Concluded

3. *Omit "00" in the cents column.*

	SIZE		TOTAL
	S	L	

4.

Name ______________________

PROBLEM 17 - 6 ___

1.

PROBLEM 17 - 6 ___ , Concluded

2.

Name ______________________________

PROBLEM 18 - 1 ___

1.

	UNIT SALES, YEAR ENDED 2000		INCREASE (DECREASE) ACTUAL OVER BUDGET	
	BUDGET	ACTUAL	AMOUNT	PERCENT

2.

	2000 ACTUAL UNITS	PERCENTAGE INCREASE (DECREASE)	2001 BUDGETED UNITS

3.

Sales Budget

For Year Ending December 31, 2001

PRODUCT AND AREA	UNIT SALES VOLUME	UNIT SELLING PRICE	TOTAL SALES

Name ______________________

PROBLEM 18 - 2 ___

1.

Sales Budget

PRODUCT AND AREA	UNIT SALES VOLUME	UNIT SELLING PRICE	TOTAL SALES

2.

Production Budget

	UNITS	

3.

Direct Materials Purchases Budget

	DIRECT MATERIALS				TOTAL

4.

Direct Labor Cost Budget

				TOTAL

Name ____________________

PROBLEM 18 - 3 ___

1.

Sales Budget

PRODUCT	UNIT SALES VOLUME	UNIT SELLING PRICE	TOTAL SALES

2.

Production Budget

	UNITS	

PROBLEM 18 - 3 ___ , Continued

3.

Direct Materials Purchases Budget

	DIRECT MATERIALS		
			TOTAL

4.

Direct Labor Cost Budget

			TOTAL

5.

Factory Overhead Cost Budget

PROBLEM 18 - 3 ___ , Continued

6.

Cost of Goods Sold Budget

7.

Selling and Administrative Expenses Budget

PROBLEM 18 - 3 ___ , Concluded

8.

Budgeted Income Statement

Name ______________________________

PROBLEM 18 - 4 ___

1. *Omit "00" in the cents columns.*

Cash Budget

PROBLEM 18 - 4 ___ , Concluded

Computations

2.

Name ______________________________

PROBLEM 18 - 5 ___

1. *Omit "00" in the cents columns.*

Budgeted Income Statement

PROBLEM 18 - 5 ___ , Concluded

2. *Omit "00" in the cents columns.*

Budgeted Balance Sheet

Name ______________________________

PROBLEM 19 - 1 ___

PROBLEM 19 - 1 ___ , Concluded

Name ______________________________

PROBLEM 19 - 2 ___

1. a. *Omit "00" in the cents columns.*

			TOTAL

PROBLEM 19 - 2 ___ , Concluded

1. b. *Omit "00" in the cents columns.*

			TOTAL

2.

Name ______________________________

PROBLEM 19 - 3 ___

a.

b.

PROBLEM 19 - 3 ___ , Concluded

c.

Name ______________________________

PROBLEM 19 - 4 ___

Factory Overhead Cost Variance Report—

Normal capacity for the month:

Actual production for the month:

	BUDGET	ACTUAL	VARIANCES FAVORABLE	VARIANCES UNFAVORABLE

Page Not Used.

Name ______________________________

PROBLEM 19 - 5 ___

PROBLEM 19 - 5 ___ , Concluded

Name ____________________

PROBLEM 20 - 1 ___

1.

PROBLEM 20 - 1 ___ , Concluded

2.

Name ____________________

PROBLEM 20 - 2 ___

1.

PROBLEM 20 - 2 ___ , Concluded

2.

3.

Name ____________________

PROBLEM 20 - 3 ___

1.

PROBLEM 20 - 3 ___ , Concluded

2.

3.

Name ______________________

PROBLEM 20 - 4 ___

1.

2.

PROBLEM 20 - 4 ___ , Concluded

3.

4.

5.

Name ___

PROBLEM 20 - 5 ___

1.

2.

3.

4.

Name ______________________________

PROBLEM 20 - 6 ___

1.

2.

PROBLEM 20 - 6 ___ , Continued

3.

			TOTAL

Name ____________________

4.

5.

PROBLEM 20 - 6 ___ , Concluded

Name ____________________

PROBLEM 21 - 1 ___

1. *Omit "00" in the cents column.*

Proposal to Operate Warehouse

2.

3.

PROBLEM 21 - 1 ___ , Concluded

Name ______________________________

PROBLEM 21 - 2 ___

1. *Omit "00" in the cents column.*

Proposal to Replace Machine

2.

Name ______________________

PROBLEM 21 - 3 ___

1. *Omit "00" in the cents column.*

Proposals for Sales Promotion Campaign

PROBLEM 21 - 3 ___ , Concluded

2.

Name ____________________

PROBLEM 21 - 4 ___

1. *Omit "00" in the cents column.*

Proposal to Process ____________________ Further

2.

Page Not Used.

Name ____________________

PROBLEM 21 - 5 ___

1.

2.

3.

PROBLEM 21 - 5 ___ , Concluded

4.

5.

6. a. *Omit "00" in the cents column.*

Proposal to Sell to

6. b.

Name ______________________________

PROBLEM 21 - 6 ___

1. *Omit "00" in the cents column.*

2.

PROBLEM 21 - 6 ___ , Concluded

3.

Name ______________________________

PROBLEM 22 - 1 ___

1. a.

1. b.

Year	Present Value of $1 at ______%	Net Cash Flow		Present Value of Net Cash Flow	
		Project _____	Project _____	Project _____	Project _____
1					
2					
3					
4					
5					
Total					
Amount to be invested					
Net present value					

2.

PROBLEM 22 - 1 ___ , Concluded

Name ____________________

PROBLEM 22 - 2 ___

1. a.

____

____

____

____

____

1. b.

Year	Present Value of $1 at ______%	Net Cash Flow		Present Value of Net Cash Flow	
		Project _____	Project _____	Project _____	Project _____
1					
2					
3					
4					
5					
Total					
Amount to be invested					
Net present value					

2.

____

____

____

____

____

____

____

____

____

____

____

____

____

____

____

____

____

____

____

PROBLEM 22 - 2 ___ , Concluded

Name ______________________________

PROBLEM 22 - 3 ___

1. Proposal (Project) _____:

Year	Present Value of $1 at _______%	Net Cash Flow	Present Value of Net Cash Flow
1			
2			
3			
Total			
Amount to be invested			
Net present value			

Proposal (Project) _____:

Year	Present Value of $1 at _______%	Net Cash Flow	Present Value of Net Cash Flow
1			
2			
3			
Total			
Amount to be invested			
Net present value			

Proposal (Project) _____:

Year	Present Value of $1 at _______%	Net Cash Flow	Present Value of Net Cash Flow
1			
2			
3			
Total			
Amount to be invested			
Net present value			

2.

3.

Name ____________________

PROBLEM 22 - 4 ___

1.

PROBLEM 22 - 4 ___ , Concluded

2.

3.

Name ______________________________

PROBLEM 22 - 5 ___

1. ______________________________

2.

Year	Present Value of $1 at _______%	Net Cash Flow		Present Value of Net Cash Flow	
		Project _____	Project _____	Project _____	Project _____
1					
2					
3					
4					
Residual value					
Total					
Amount to be invested					
Net present value					

PROBLEM 22 - 5 ___ , Concluded

3.

Name ____________________

PROBLEM 22 - 6 ___

1.

2.

3.

Proposal	Cash Payback Period	Average Rate of Return	Accept for Further Analysis	Reject
A				
B				
C				
D				

4. Proposal ___:

Year	Present Value of $1 at _______%	Net Cash Flow	Present Value of Net Cash Flow
1			
2			
3			
4			
5			
Total			
Amount to be invested			
Net present value			

Proposal ___:

Year	Present Value of $1 at _______%	Net Cash Flow	Present Value of Net Cash Flow
1			
2			
3			
4			
5			
Total			
Amount to be invested			
Net present value			

PROBLEM 22 - 6 ___ , Concluded

5.

6.

7.

8.

Name ______________________

PROBLEM 23 - 1 ___

1.

2.

PROBLEM 23 - 1 ___ , Concluded

Name ____________________

PROBLEM 23 - 2 ___

1.

2.

PROBLEM 23 - 2 ___ , Concluded

Name ______________________________

PROBLEM 23 - 3 ___

1.

2.

	DIRECT LABOR HOURS	X	PRODUCTION DEPARTMENT RATE	=	FACTORY OVERHEAD

3.

PROBLEM 23 - 3 ___ , Concluded

4.

	ACTIVITY-BASE USAGE	X ACTIVITY RATE	= ACTIVITY COST

5.

Name ____________________

PROBLEM 23 - 4 ___

1. and 3.

PROBLEM 23 - 4 ___ , Concluded

2.

	ACTIVITY-BASE USAGE	X ACTIVITY RATE	= ACTIVITY COST

Name ____________________

PROBLEM 23 - 5 ___

1. ____________________

2. ____________________

PROBLEM 23 - 5 ___ , Continued

3.

4.

Page Not Used.

Name ______________________

PROBLEM 23 - 6 ___

1.

2.

PROBLEM 23 - 6 ___ , Concluded

3.

4.

Name ______________________

PROBLEM 24 - 1 ___

1. ______________________

2. ______________________

PROBLEM 24 - 1 ___ , Concluded

3.

Name ____________________

PROBLEM 24 - 2 ___

1.

PROBLEM 24 - 2 ___ , Concluded

2.

Name ______________________

PROBLEM 24 - 3 ___

1. ______________________

2. ______________________

3.

JOURNAL PAGE

	DATE		DESCRIPTION	POST. REF.	DEBIT	CREDIT	
1							1
2							2
3							3
4							4
5							5
6							6
7							7
8							8
9							9
10							10
11							11
12							12
13							13
14							14
15							15
16							16
17							17
18							18
19							19
20							20
21							21
22							22
23							23
24							24
25							25
26							26
27							27

4.

5.

Name ______________________________

PROBLEM 24 - 4 ___

1.

Dollars

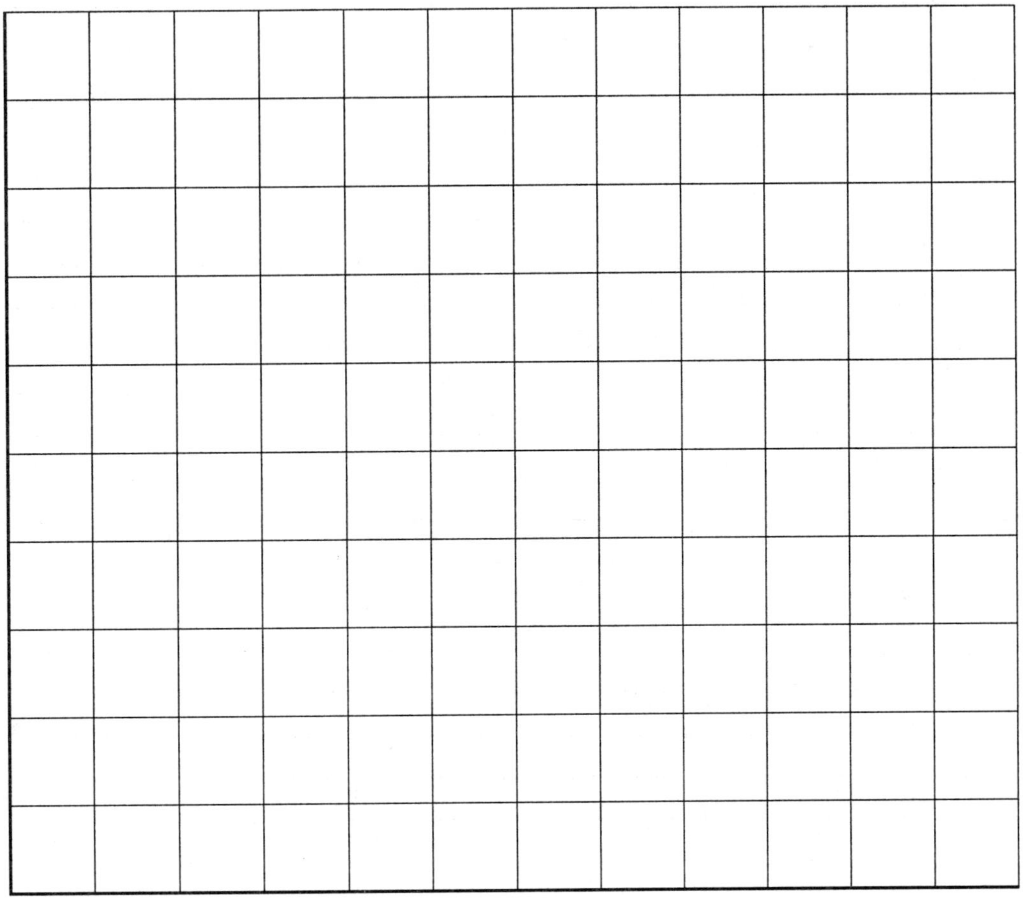

Activity Categories

PROBLEM 24 - 4 ___ , Concluded

2., 3., and 4.

Name ______________________

PROBLEM SCF - 1 ___

Omit "00" in the cents columns.

PROBLEM SCF - 1 ___ , Continued

Name ____________________

PROBLEM SCF - 1 ___ , Continued

The use of this form is not required unless so indicated by the instructor.

Work Sheet for Statement of Cash Flows

ACCOUNTS	BALANCE, ________ , 1999	TRANSACTIONS		BALANCE, ________ , 2000
		DEBIT	CREDIT	

PROBLEM SCF - 1 ___ , Concluded

ACCOUNTS	BALANCE, ________, 1999	TRANSACTIONS		BALANCE, ________, 2000
		DEBIT	CREDIT	

Name ______________________________

PROBLEM SCF - 2 ___

Omit "00" in the cents columns.

PROBLEM SCF - 2 ___ , Continued

Name ______________________________

PROBLEM SCF - 2 ___ , Continued

The use of this form is not required unless so indicated by the instructor.

Work Sheet for Statement of Cash Flows

ACCOUNTS	BALANCE, DEC. 31, 1999	TRANSACTIONS		BALANCE, DEC. 31, 2000
		DEBIT	CREDIT	

PROBLEM SCF - 2 ___ , Concluded

ACCOUNTS	BALANCE, DEC. 31, 1999	TRANSACTIONS		BALANCE, DEC. 31, 2000
		DEBIT	CREDIT	

Name ___________________________

PROBLEM SCF - 3 ___

Omit "00" in the cents columns.

PROBLEM SCF - 3 ___ , Continued

Name ____________________

PROBLEM SCF - 3 ___ , Continued

The use of this form is not required unless so indicated by the instructor.

Work Sheet for Statement of Cash Flows

ACCOUNTS	BALANCE, DEC. 31, 1999	TRANSACTIONS		BALANCE, DEC. 31, 2000
		DEBIT	CREDIT	

PROBLEM SCF - 3 ___ , Concluded

ACCOUNTS	BALANCE, DEC. 31, 1999	TRANSACTIONS		BALANCE, DEC, 31, 2000
		DEBIT	CREDIT	

Name ______________________________

PROBLEM SCF - 4 ___

Omit "00" in the cents columns.

PROBLEM SCF - 4 ___ , Continued

Name ____________________

PROBLEM SCF - 4 ___ , Continued

The use of this form is not required unless so indicated by the instructor.

Work Sheet for Statement of Cash Flows

ACCOUNTS	BALANCE, DEC. 31, 2000	TRANSACTIONS		BALANCE, DEC. 31, 2001
		DEBIT	CREDIT	

PROBLEM SCF - 4 ___ , Concluded

ACCOUNTS	BALANCE, DEC. 31, 2000	TRANSACTIONS		BALANCE, DEC. 31, 2001
		DEBIT	CREDIT	

Name ______________________________

PROBLEM SCF - 5 ___

Omit "00" in the cents columns.

PROBLEM SCF - 5 ___ , Continued

Name ____________________

PROBLEM SCF - 5 ___ , Continued

The use of this form is not required unless so indicated by the instructor.

Work Sheet for Statement of Cash Flows

ACCOUNTS	BALANCE, ________, 1999	TRANSACTIONS DEBIT	TRANSACTIONS CREDIT	BALANCE, ________, 2000

PROBLEM SCF - 5 ___ , Concluded

ACCOUNTS	BALANCE, ________, 1999	TRANSACTIONS		BALANCE, ________, 2000
		DEBIT	CREDIT	

Name ______________________________

PROBLEM FSA - 1 ___

1.

Comparative Income Statement

	2000	1999	INCREASE (DECREASE)	
			AMOUNT	PERCENT

PROBLEM FSA - 1 ___ , Concluded

2.

Name ______________________________

PROBLEM FSA - 2 ___

1.

Comparative Income Statement

	2000		1999	
	AMOUNT	PERCENT	AMOUNT	PERCENT

PROBLEM FSA - 2 ___ , Concluded

2.

Name ______________________________

PROBLEM FSA - 3 ___

1.a.

1.b.

1.c.

PROBLEM FSA - 3 ___ , Concluded

2.

Transaction	Working Capital	Current Ratio	Acid-Test Ratio
a.			
b.			
c.			
d.			
e.			
f.			
g.			
h.			
i.			
j.			

Name ____________________

PROBLEM FSA - 4 ___

1. through 19.

PROBLEM FSA - 4 ___ , Concluded

Name ____________________

PROBLEM FSA - 5 ___

1. a.

PROBLEM FSA - 5 ___ , Continued

1. b.

Name ______________________________

PROBLEM FSA - 5 ___ , Continued

1. c.

1. d.

Name ______________________________

PROBLEM FSA - 5 ___ , Continued

2.

Name

HERSHEY FOODS CORPORATION PROBLEM

1. a. through r.

2.

Name

Extra Forms

JOURNAL

PAGE

	DATE	DESCRIPTION	POST. REF.	DEBIT	CREDIT	
1						1
2						2
3						3
4						4
5						5
6						6
7						7
8						8
9						9
10						10
11						11
12						12
13						13
14						14
15						15
16						16
17						17
18						18
19						19
20						20
21						21
22						22
23						23
24						24
25						25
26						26
27						27
28						28
29						29
30						30
31						31
32						32
33						33

JOURNAL

PAGE

	DATE	DESCRIPTION	POST. REF.	DEBIT	CREDIT	
1						1
2						2
3						3
4						4
5						5
6						6
7						7
8						8
9						9
10						10
11						11
12						12
13						13
14						14
15						15
16						16
17						17
18						18
19						19
20						20
21						21
22						22
23						23
24						24
25						25
26						26
27						27
28						28
29						29
30						30
31						31
32						32
33						33

Name ______________________________

Extra Forms

JOURNAL

PAGE ____

	DATE		DESCRIPTION	POST. REF.	DEBIT	CREDIT	
1							1
2							2
3							3
4							4
5							5
6							6
7							7
8							8
9							9
10							10
11							11
12							12
13							13
14							14
15							15
16							16
17							17
18							18
19							19
20							20
21							21
22							22
23							23
24							24
25							25
26							26
27							27
28							28
29							29
30							30
31							31
32							32
33							33

JOURNAL

PAGE

	DATE		DESCRIPTION	POST. REF.	DEBIT	CREDIT	
1							1
2							2
3							3
4							4
5							5
6							6
7							7
8							8
9							9
10							10
11							11
12							12
13							13
14							14
15							15
16							16
17							17
18							18
19							19
20							20
21							21
22							22
23							23
24							24
25							25
26							26
27							27
28							28
29							29
30							30
31							31
32							32
33							33

Name ______________________________

Extra Forms

Extra Forms

Name ______________________________

Extra Forms

Name ____________________

Extra Forms

Name ______________________________

Extra Forms